School Poems

Compiled by

Jennifer Curry

Illustrated by

Kate Sheppard

Hippo

This book is for RUTH HATTERSLEY,
my very special reading and writing friend,
with my love.

Scholastic Children's Books,
Commonwealth House, 1-19 New Oxford Street,
London WC1A 1NU, UK
A division of Scholastic Ltd
London ~ New York ~ Toronto ~ Sydney ~ Auckland
Mexico City ~ New Delhi ~ Hong Kong

First published in the UK by Scholastic Ltd, 1999
This edition published by Scholastic Ltd, 2005

ISBN 0 439 95972 1

Printed by Nørhaven Paperback A/S, Denmark.

2 4 6 8 10 9 7 5 3 1

CONTENTS

School Calendar 3

The Classroom Circle

School Calendar 1

Back to School Blues

Late August,
The miserable countdown starts,
Millions of kids
With lead in their hearts.
In Woolies' window: rubbers, rulers,
Geometry sets,
And a BACK TO SCHOOL sign –
I mean, who forgets?
In the clothes shops
Ghastly models of kids with
New satchels and blazers and shoes:
Enough to give anybody
Those Back to School Blues.

And Auntie Nell from Liverpool,
Who's down with us for a visit,
Smiles and says, "So it's back to school
On Wednesday for you, is it?
I only wish I'd got the chance

Of my schooldays over again...
Happiest days of my life they were –
Though I didn't realize it then..."
And she rabbits on like that,
Just twisting away at the screws;
She's forgotten about
The Back to School Blues.

And six and a half long weeks
Have melted away like ice-cream:
That Costa Brava fortnight's
Vanished like a dream.
And Dad says, "Look, this term
At school, could you try and do
A bit better?
For a start you could learn to spell
And write a decent letter.
And just keep away from that Hazel Stephens –
She's total bad news..."
Any wonder that I've got
Those Back to School Blues?

Eric Finney

The Very First Day

Kindergarten

Sun is shining...

Me dey ya in dis place wid dese strange faces. An'
me alone.

Sun is shining
me have tuppence in me pocket...

Me dey ya in dis place wid dese strange faces. An'
me alone.
An' me can't do wha me want. An' me wan' go
home.

Sun is shining
me have tuppence in me pocket
me have two banana...

Me dey ya in dis place wid dese strange faces. An'
   me alone. An' me can't do wha' me want. An'
      me wan' go home.
Me muma leave me and gone far away. An' a wan'
   see her.
Me wan' go to market, me don't wan' be wid dese
   strange people. Me wan' go home.

Sun is shining
me have tuppence in me pocket
me have two banana

me have ball...

But watchya now: we playing, we dancing, we singing.
   An' de big people nice. Dem show me nice t'ings...

Stanley Martin

First Day at School

My new friend and I
  feel a bit scared,
But things are easier
  when they're shared.

Charles Thomson

School Calendar 2

Treat or Trick?

The head said we could decorate
Our school this Hallowe'en –
Then gave us white emulsion paint
And brushes – ain't he mean!

Philip Waddell

The Long School Day

Here it Comes!

Hear the shouts
Hear the cries
It's the morning slanging match
It's late homework
Time to tease
Lost boots
Banged knees
Sharing secrets
Telling jokes
It's the top
Gossip shop
An eruption
When it stops
It's...
The school bus!

Patricia Leighton

At the End of School Assembly

Miss Sparrow's lot flew out,
Mrs Steed's lot galloped out,
Mr Bull's lot got herded out,
Mrs Bumble's lot buzzed off.

Miss Rose's class ... rose,
Mr Beetle's class ... beetled off,
Miss Storm's class thundered out,
Mrs Frisby's class whirled across the hall.

Mr Train's lot made tracks,
Miss Ferry's lot sailed off,
Mr Roller's lot got their skates on,
Mrs Street's lot got stuck halfway across.

Mr Idle's class couldn't be bothered,
Mrs Barrow's class were wheeled out,
Miss Stretcher's class were carried out,
And
Mrs Brook's class
Simply
Trickled away

Simon Pitt

Best Lesson

It was the best lesson ever
the first of the week,
the children didn't say a word
the teacher didn't speak.

The chairs didn't scrape
as everyone walked in slow,
gazing out from misted glass
at a magic world of snow.

Andrew Collett

Colour of my Dreams

I'm a really rotten reader
the worst in all the class,
the sort of rotten reader
that makes you want to laugh.

I'm last in all the readin' tests,
my score's not on the page
and when I read to teacher
she gets in such a rage.

She says I cannot form my words
she says I can't build up
and that I don't know phonics
– and don't know c-a-t from k-u-p.

They say that I'm dyslexic
(that's a word they've just found out)
... but when I get some plasticine
I know what that's about.

I make these scary monsters
I draw these secret lands
and get my hair all sticky
and paint on all me hands.

I make these super models,
I build these smashing towers
that reach up to the ceiling
– and take me hours and hours.

I paint these lovely pictures
in thick green drippy paint
that gets all on the carpet –
and makes the cleaners faint.

I build great magic forests
weave bushes out of string
and paint pink panderellos
and birds that really sing.

I play my world of real believe
I play it every day
and teachers stand and watch me
but don't know what to say.

They give me diagnostic tests,
they try out reading schemes,
but none of them will ever know
the colour of my dreams.

Peter Dixon

Giggles

Aggle, waggle,
I write "a".

Eggle, weggle,
I write "e".

Iggle, wiggle,
I write "i".

Oggle, woggle,
I write "o".

Uggle, wuggle,
I write "u".

Daniel Bishop (6)

There's Someone in our Class...

There's someone. In our class who cannot.
Write in sentences our. Teacher keeps saying
write. In decent sentences a sentence is.
A group of words that makes complete. Sense.
But this. Someone never. Listens!

Their's somion inn or clas ho canknot spel
proupirlei.
He as the mosst auful spileing nowlidge.
Mrs Catlledinner ses it's dubble ditch.
But thiss somion niver lissteenss!

There'ssomeoneinourclasswhoneverleavesafinger
spacebetweenwords.MrsCastledinedoesnotapprove
ofhiswriting.Shesayshemusthaveeverythinfingers.
Butthissomeoneneverlistens.

There's someone in our class
who writes too big.
He tries to write small
but he hasn't got the knack yet.
This someone is a very small person –
not like his writing!

There's someone in our class who cannot
concentrate.
This someone finds it very difficult to...

"What was I saying?"

Marcus Throup (11)

Fox

Midwinter, mid-morning
Of a dark-grey day.
Outside snow settles
On a playground
Where we won't be allowed to play.

We're inside, in the warm
Classroom, listening
As Miss reads poems...
One where a fox
Comes trotting, green eyes glistening,

Out of a midnight forest,
Into a poet's mind.
I see it clearly:
Sharp ears, long snout,
Red soft fur stirring in the wind...

The poem's called "The Thought Fox".
Miss says it's a great
Way of capturing
A fox in words.
Then I see it at the school gate.

There, where the bushes hide
Overflowing bins.
I hold my breath, stare
Through the window
And feel a tingling in my skin.

The fox breathes steam. It's real,
A city creature
Forced out in daylight
To scavenge scraps.
It stands proud, beyond our teacher.

"Miss!" someone hisses. "It's
By the gate, just look!"
But Miss keeps reading,
Takes no notice,
Eyes fixed on the pages of her book.

Whispers grow, till at last
Miss crossly turns, peers
Where we're all pointing,
But she's too late.
A swift red shadow disappears.

Miss tuts, and blames our strong
Imaginations,
The poem's power.
She looks away,
Happy with her explanation.

Picks up where she left off...
But the trail is cold.
Outside snow settles,
Slowly covers
The tracks that show a fox was bold.

Tony Bradman

Playground Fight

It was me and him,
I charged,
he ducked,
I ran into a brick wall,
I bounced back,
and hit him on the head,
he fell to the floor,
I squashed him,
I took him home,
and put him through the letter-box,
because he was flat.
The next day he came back,
flat as a pancake,
he wobbled,
he became himself again,
he charged,
I stuck out my fist,
he ran into it...
the headmaster came,
we got detention.

Raymond Trott (10)

A Quick Way of Counting to 100

1, 2,
skip a few,
99, 100.

Anon

Maths my Way

Two plus two is twenty-two.
It's plain as day that this is true.
But teacher says she's very sure
That two plus two adds up to four.

Three plus three makes thirty-three.
That's the way it ought to be.
But teacher says the answer's six.
I don't know why. Must be a trick.

Four plus four is forty-four.
Not any less, not any more.
My teacher just can't get it straight.
She keeps on saying the answer's eight.

I give up. I'll go along.
I'll do it her way, though she's wrong.
But in my heart, I know what's true –
Two plus two makes twenty-two.

Carol Diggory Shields

Ten School Computers

Ten school computers all on line:
one went down, and then there were nine.

Nine school computers, until my mate
blew one up, and then there were eight.

Eight school computers, but one was loaned from
  Devon
and had to be returned, and then there were
  seven.

Seven school computers, but one always sticks,
so that was no good, and then there were six.

Six school computers, but one belonged to Clive
and he took it home, and then there were five.

Five school computers, but one fell on the floor
and then it wouldn't work, and then there were
  four.

Four school computers, but one's for class B,
so we couldn't use that one, and then there were
  three.

Three school computers, till someone spilt some
  glue
which gummed one up, and then there were two.

Two school computers, one was left in the sun
and it burst into flames, and then there was one.

One school computer. "Children, DON'T RUN!"
Bang, crash, tinkle ... and then there were none!

Charles Thomson

Song of the Starving Dinner Ladies

Green flies, gulls' beaks, gizzard of gnu,
mix them well Mrs Stodge,
we want a lovely sticky stew.

Rubber bands, bits of string sprinkled with
   confetti,
stir the pot well Mrs Slop,
we'll convince them it's spaghetti.

Dollops of yellow Dulux paint, fluff off a duster,
simmer very gently Mrs Sludge,
we don't want lumpy custard!

John Rice

Paul's Flowers

The clock said two; the iron
School-bell had ceased to clank,
When Paul lingered to pick
Three dandelions on the bank.

No children in the school-yard;
None by the gate.
He pushed the class-door open
And saw that he was late.

All eyed him. Paul came forward
With hesitating foot,
Laid his three flowers in the teacher's
Lap and was mute.

Then in the shocked stillness
Teacher began to scold...
But Paul, his eyes turned downward
To her dress's fold,
Saw those three flowers had grown
To a strange gold.

Strange gold that breathed a petalled
Warmth on the air!
And one black midge that basked
In summer there!

With shut ears Paul watched it –
Shut ears and bended head –
Till teacher's voice had faded;
And, "Take your flowers!" she said.

Paul to his desk has gone,
Silent, and on his knee
Holding the three bright dandelions
Miserably.

John Walsh

Fruit

Some things are true
And some are only true in school.

Like fruit. We did fruit
Today in Science. We learnt

A tomato's fruit but
A strawberry isn't.

I copied down the diagrams
And all the notes —

'Cos I knew I had to
Pretend it was true.

I'm not daft, I know when
To make believe:

That's why I'm
Set One for Science.

Mick Gowar

M is for Mango

Outside – the hot sun shining bright,
Inside – our class learning to write,
We are spelling m-a-n-g-o,
We are smelling mango –
Outside – hanging easy-reach height.

Outside – Sam is sucking a seed,
Inside – all together we read,
We chant *"Mangoes are sweet*
And delicious to eat" –
Outside – Sam is doing the deed.

Outside – it's a ripe mango day,
Inside – we learn "taking away"
With ... *three mangoes from four?*
I can't take any more
...Miss PLEASE can we go out to play?

Philip Waddell

Infant Art

Paint on the ceiling
Paint in my hair
Paint on the table
Paint on my chair
Paint all around me
Paint *everywhere* –
Except on my paper
There's no paint there.

Jennifer Curry

Ten Cornflowers

Wednesday is Art. My favourite day.
Or used to be until the cornflowers.
Ten cornflowers in a jar. I loved them,
Burning blue. Impatient to begin
I scoured my paintbox. Cobalt. Azure
And Prussian Blue. I mixed them well,
And laid them on my page, and saw
The flowers bloom beneath my brush.
I showed my friend. "Dad grows these in
Our garden. Mam's special flower, the colour
Of her eyes." The teacher pounced.
"Time to talk? No need to work?
Perhaps you'll show us what you've done?"
She held my painting to the class,
While I sat proudly by. But then,
"Now children look at this," she said,
"And learn how NOT to paint. Jane
Calls them flowers. But what do we see?
Just ten green sticks in a crooked jar,
And ten awful blobs of horrible blue."

Wednesday is always Art. It was my favourite day,
But now, if I can manage it, I try to stay away.

Jenny Craig

First School Days

The school days seem ever so l-o-n-g –
longer than a dinosaur's tongue
When you're little and   alone.
The mornings must be timed by a giant's clock,
with an ever so so so slow tick tock.
And I yawn in the huge afternoons

Tim Pointon

Storytime

Once upon a time, children,
there lived a fearsome dragon...

Please Miss, Jamie's made a dragon.
Out in the sandpit.

Lovely, Andrew.
Now this dragon
had enormous red eyes
and a swirling, whirling tail...

Jamie's dragon's got
yellow eyes, Miss.

Lovely, Andrew.
Now this dragon was
as wide as a horse
as green as the grass
as tall as a house...

Jamie's would JUST fit
in our classroom, Miss!

But he was a very friendly dragon...

Jamie's dragon ISN'T, Miss.
He eats people, Miss.
Especially TEACHERS,
Jamie said.

Very nice, Andrew!
Now one day, children,
this enormous dragon
rolled his red eye,
whirled his swirly green tail
and set off to find...

His dinner, Miss!
Because he was hungry, Miss!

Thank you, Andrew.
He rolled his red eye,
whirled his green tail,
and opened his wide, wide mouth
until o

    o

     o

    o

   o

Please Miss,
I did try to
tell you, Miss!

  o   u

   o   u

    o o O

Judith Nicholls

42

Mr Piper

When Mr Piper came to our school
we gawped at his clothes
and said, "Cor! Cool!
Just look at those colours.
Wow, crazy kit!"
Then gradually got used to it.

When Mr Piper took out his whistle
we all sat up and whispered, "This'll
be fun." But then the head came in
and called out, "Piper, what's this din?
Ah, music lessons ... a fine pursuit.
I wish that I could play the flute.
Carry on, carry on. They could do
with some tuning, this lot..."

When Mr Piper marched away
we all jumped up and called, "Hooray!"
and danced out into the air and sun
and followed him, yes everyone,
and dropped our pens
and left our books
and gym-kit dangling down from hooks,
and danced away across the grass
leaving a silent empty class.

And as we left,
the head was heard to say,
"The things these teachers teach today!"

Tony Mitton

At the End of a School Day

It is the end of a school day
  and down the long driveway
come bag-swinging, shouting children.
  Deafened, the sky winces.
    The sun gapes in surprise.

Suddenly the runners skid to a stop,
  stand still and stare
at a small hedgehog
  curled up on the tarmac
    like an old, frayed cricket ball.

A girl dumps her bag, tiptoes forward
  and gingerly, so gingerly
carries the creature
  to the safety of a shady hedge.
    Then steps back, watching.

Girl, children, sky and sun
  hold their breath.
There is a silence,
  a moment to remember
    on this warm afternoon in June.

Wes Magee

45

Moonwalker

I'm a moonwalker, walking on the moon.
I'm a jungle stalker, stalking wild baboons.
I'm a superhero, skimming through the blue.
Puddle jumping, leaf-pile leaping, I'm a kangaroo.

I'm a desert rattlesnake, sliding through the sand.
Counting out the beat, I'm the leader of the band.
I'm Tyrannosaurus, looking for a snack.
Whoo-whoo! I'm a train, rolling down the track.

I'm a red-eyed robot, clanking up the road.
I'm an eighteen-wheeler with a heavy load.
I'm a famous rock star, moving very cool.
Actually,
  I'm just me,
    Walking home from school.

Carol Diggory Shields

46

Plodders

We homeward plod, our satchels full
Of books to make our evenings dull.
We homeward plod, our heads hung low,
Crammed full of facts One Ought To Know.

Tomorrow we will plod once more
To school, where we will stay till four,
Or thereabouts, for that is when,
With books, we'll homeward plod again.

Colin West

Jazzz Watches Candy
do her Homework

Jazzz watches Candy
do her homework.
It's school work she does
at home
to help her work better
in school.

First
she drinks a can of Coke.
Then
she eats a bag of crisps.
Then
she takes the ribbon
out of her hair.
Then
she bites her nails.
Then
she hangs upside down
in the chair.
Then
she writes a word
upside down in her book.
Then
she breaks her pencil
and has to sharpen it.

Then
she puts her ribbon back in.
Then
she drinks another
can of Coke.
Then
she hangs upside down
in the chair
again.
Then she writes the next letter
of the next word.
And then
she finds
a piece of wool
to throw for Jazzz
to chase.

So
Jazzz never sees
what she does next.

But
homework seems to be
lots of fun.
And if homework
is really school work,
Jazzz wishes
he could go to school.

                                    Dave Ward

School Calendar 3

Looking Forward to Divali

Divali light
will cheer the dark
November night.

We decorate
the classroom wall
to celebrate.

Each Hindu
hears Rama's tale
and knows it's true.

Be joyful then.
Our festival
is here again.

Ann Bonner

The Classroom Circle

The Classroom Circle
of Friends

and I like Anne

Dan likes me → I like Anne

Dee likes Dan   Anne likes John

Titch likes Dee   John likes Mike

Mo likes Titch   Mike likes Ron

Mitch likes Mo   Ron likes Paul

Ray likes Mitch   Paul likes Pam

Bert likes Ray   Pam likes Jack

George likes Bert   Jack likes Sam

Gert likes George   Sam likes Jane

Jock likes Gert   Jane likes Rick

Faye likes Jock   Rick likes Jo

Chris likes Faye   Jo likes Mick

May likes Chris   Mick likes Val

Ken likes May   Val likes Jill

Phil likes Ken   Jill likes Trish

Trish likes Phil

(→ start here)

Wes Magee

51

Photographs

I have only been in the paper once,
At my first school,
The photograph was long,
Long and thin,
I was second from the end.
I stood there smiling
Waiting for the trigger to click
My friend was next to me,
Waiting too.
Then it clicked
And the photograph was taken.
Next day, there we were
In the paper.
A humble little school,
In the long, thin photograph.
With me there,
Next to my friend,
In the only picture in the paper,
In my life.

Nicholas Grant (10)

My Favourite Job

I love sharpening pencils.
I love the way the wood
comes off in curly strips
like thin flat worms.

I love to see the new wood
coming through
and all the dirty wood
shaved clean away.

I love the smell –
it's like a mini-autumn!
Reminds me of conkers
and bonfire nights.

I love it when they're finished
and all in the pencil rack,
a rainbow of brilliant colours,
all the king's men on parade!

But best of all is when Sir
pats my shoulder and says
*"You've made a good job of that, Shaun.
Thanks."*

                                        Patricia Leighton

New Leaf

Today is the first day of my new book.
I've written the date
and underlined it
in red felt-tip
with a ruler.
I'm going to be different
with this book.
With this book

I'm going to be good.
With this book
I'm always going to do the date like that
dead neat
with a ruler
just like Christine Robinson.

With this book
I'll be as clever as Graham Holden,
get all my sums right, be as
neat as Mark Veitch;
I'll keep my pens and pencils
in a pencil case
and never have to borrow again.

With this book
I'm going to work hard,
not talk, be different –
with this book,
not yell out, mess about,
be silly –
with this book.

With this book
I'll be grown-up, sensible,
and everyone will want me;
I'll be picked out first
like Iain Cartwright:
no one will ever laugh at me again.
Everything will be
different

with this book...

Mick Gowar

Emma and Rebbecca

Emma and Rebbecca sit behind us,
And oh, the fuss,
"That's my pen." "Oh no it's mine."
"Shut up Emma." "Shut up yourself."
"What's your phone number?" "What's yours?"
"Ain't gonna tell ya."
"Won't tell you mine, then."
"Fine."
"OK, let's work now."
"OK."
And I say, "Shut up you pair," and they say
"Don't tell me, tell her!"

Kelly Bambrick (10)

Quarrel

He didn't call for me on the way to school,
I played with somebody else.

I sat with someone else in assembly,
He looked upset but angry coming out.

I found a felt-pen mark on my English book,
I put biro on his jumper.

I nudged him so his pencil slipped,
He nudged me and my pen slipped.

He fouled me in soccer,
I belted the ball at him.

He put yellow paint in my red,
I put yellow in his black.

I think he poked his tongue out at me,
I gently touched him.

He walked home with me as usual,
I called for him to see if he would play.

Jeremy Consitt (11)

Serious Luv

Monday Morning
I really luv de girl dat's sitting next to me
I think she thinks like me an she's so cool,
I think dat we could live for ever happily
I want to marry her when I leave school.

She's de only one in school allowed to call me
  Ben
When she does Maths I luv de way she chews her
  pen,
When we are doing Art she's so artistic
In Biology she makes me heart beat so quick.

When we do Geography I go to paradise
She's helped me draw a map of Borneo twice!
Today she's going to help me take me books home
So I am going to propose to her when we're
  alone.

The Next Day

I used to luv de girl dat's sitting next to me
But yesterday it all came to an end,
She said that I should take love more seriously
An now I think I really luv her friend.

Benjamin Zephaniah

Bully for You

"I'm glad, really glad, I'm not (urrr) *you*!
In fact everybody in this playground,
will be really glad, they're not (urrr) *you*!
Come to think of it,
everybody in the entire universe
will be really glad, they're not (urrr) *you*!
Because when I've finished, done with, got
   through,
You aren't going to recognize,
Who? – Yes (urrr) – *you*!"

"Who, *me*?
This little slip of a *me*!
This little puff of a, snuff of a, not enough of a *me*!
This little won't hurt a flea, never mind a pea, *me*!
You are threatening *me*!
Well, bully boy,
I'm not one for much talking or squawking,
so listen very carefully,
for I'm breathing danger here!
Your name may be bully boy
but mine's *bully girl*
watcha!"

Ian Souter

A-shhoo!

Hay fever isn't at all funny.
You feel half-sick,
Your eyes are runny,
Your mouth is dry but your throat is thick.

Nice sunny day! But you start wheezing.
Your chest is sore
And now you're sneezing.
Atishhoo! Cough, and sneeze some more.

I'm dreaming, sitting here at school,
Of fresh blue sea
Or a swimming pool.
Such cool relief from this allergy.

But Teacher knows and she will say,
"You can stay in
When the others play,
And take your antihistamine."

An all-grey sky, when it rains and rains,
Washing away
The pollen grains;
That's what I would call a perfect day.

Robert Sparrow

The Truant

Tam Broon often plunkit schule,
For lessons he couldna abide,
Up tae the Myot he'd gae,
An' push aw his schule work aside.

He likit warm June best o' aw,
When the days were sae bricht and lang,
And the Carron wis bonny and blue,
An' aw the wee birds chirped an' sang.

When fitstep he heard he'd hide,
In case it was Polis or Janny,
If caught he wad stammer an say,
"O please, dinna tell my mammy."

Year Five Group Work

62

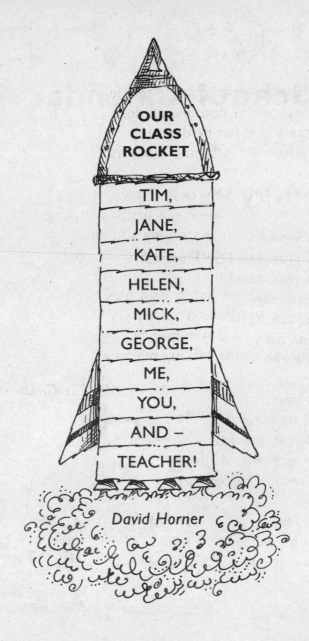

OUR
CLASS
ROCKET

TIM,

JANE,

KATE,

HELEN,

MICK,

GEORGE,

ME,

YOU,

AND –

TEACHER!

David Horner

Nativity Play

This year...
This year, can I be Herod?
This year, can I be him?
A wise man
or a Joseph?
An inn man
or a king?

This year...
can I be famous
This year, can I be best?
Bear a crown of silver
and wear a golden vest?

This year...
can I be starlight?
This year, can I stand out?

... feel the swish of curtains
and hear the front row shout
"Hurrah" for good old Ronny
he brings a gift of gold
head afire with tinsel
"The Greatest Story Told..."
"Hurrah for good old Herod!"
and shepherds from afar.

So –
don't make me a palm tree
and can I be –
                    a Star.

Peter Dixon

What Have You Got To Say For Yourself?

Schoolitis

You haven't got a cough,
You haven't got mumps,
You haven't got a chill
Or any funny lumps.
You haven't got tummy-ache,
You haven't got a fever,
You haven't got a runny nose
Or chicken-pox either.
You don't look a ruin,
You don't look a wreck,
You haven't got toothache
Or a pain in the neck.
You're as fit as a fiddle,
You're sound as a bell,
In fact I've never ever
Seen you looking so well!

You don't fool me,
I'm no fool.
Now up out of bed
AND OFF TO SCHOOL!

Brian Patten

Late

You're late, said Miss.
The bell has gone,
dinner numbers done
and work begun.

What have you got to say for yourself?

Well, it's like this, Miss
Me mum was sick,
me dad fell down the stairs,
the wheel fell off me bike
and then we lost our Billy's snake
behind the kitchen chairs. Earache
struck down me grampy, me gran
took quite a funny turn.
Then on the way I met this man
whose dog attacked me shin –
look, miss, you can see the blood,
it doesn't look too good,
does it?

Yes, yes, sit down –
and next time say you're sorry
for disturbing all the class.
Now, get on with your story,
fast!

Please Miss, I've got nothing to write about.

Judith Nicholls

Conversation Piece

Late again Blenkinsop?
What's the excuse this time?
Not my fault sir.
Who's fault is it then?
Grandma's sir.
Grandma's? What did she do?
She died sir.
Died?
She's seriously dead all right sir.
That makes four grandmothers this term.
And all on PE days Blenkinsop.
I know. It's very upsetting sir.
How many grandmothers have you got
Blenkinsop?
Grandmothers sir? None sir.
None?
All dead sir.
And what about yesterday Blenkinsop?
What about yesterday sir?
You missed maths.
That was the dentist sir.
The dentist died?
No sir. My teeth sir.
You missed the test Blenkinsop.
I'd been looking forward to it too sir.

Right, line up for PE.
Can't sir.
No such word as can't. Why can't you?
No kit sir.
Where is it?
Home sir.
What's it doing at home?
Not ironed sir.
Couldn't you iron it?
Can't do it sir.
Why not?
My hand sir.
Who usually does it?
Grandma sir.
Why couldn't she do it?
Dead sir.

Gareth Owen

A Teacher's Lament

Don't tell me the cat ate your maths sheet,
And your spelling words went down the drain,
And you couldn't decipher your homework,
Because it was soaked in the rain.

Don't tell me you slaved for hours
On the project that's due today,
And you would have had it finished
If your snake hadn't run away.

Don't tell me you lost your eraser,
And your worksheets and pencils, too,
And your papers are stuck together
With a great big glob of glue.

I'm tired of all your excuses;
They are really a terrible bore.
Besides, I forgot my own work,
At home in my study drawer.

Kalli Dakos

School Calendar 5

Our Classroom has a Mailbox

Our classroom has a mailbox
that we painted red and gold,
we stuffed it with more valentines
than it was made to hold.

When we opened it this morning
I was nervous as could be,
I wondered if a single one
had been addressed to me.

But when they'd been delivered
I felt twenty storeys tall,
I got so many valentines
I couldn't hold them all.

Jack Prelutsky

Do You Know My Teacher?

Do you Know my Teacher?

She's got a piercing stare
and long black...

  (a) moustache
  (b) hair
  (c) teeth
  (d) shoes

She eats chips and beef
and has short sharp...

  (a) nails
  (b) fangs
  (c) doorstoppers
  (d) teef

She is slinky and thin
and has a pointed...
> (a) banana
> (b) chin
> (c) beard
> (d) umbrella

She has a long straight nose
and hairy little...
> (a) kneecaps
> (b) ears
> (c) children
> (d) toes

She has sparkling eyes
and wears school...
> (a) dinners
> (b) trousers
> (c) ties
> (d) buses

She comes from down south
and has a very big...
> (a) vocabulary
> (b) handbag
> (c) bottom
> (d) mouth

She yells like a preacher
yes, that's my...
     (a) budgie
     (b) stick
     (c) padlock
     (d) teacher!

John Rice

How the New Teacher got her Nickname

When the new teacher said,
"I'm going to be frank with you,"
I burst out laughing.
"What are you laughing about?" she asked.
"It's hard to explain, Frank," I said.
From that moment on Miss Jones became Frank.
For that, she has me to thank.

Brian Patten

Miss Sweet and Sour

When our teacher's in a bad mood
She comes in hard as spite.
Her chin sticks out like a jutting crag,
Her eyes flash like gelignite.

Her neck turns red, her tongue turns sharp,
Her mouth becomes a steel trap.
Her heels click like knitting pins,
Her voice is like a thunder-clap.

But when she's in a good mood
She comes in soft as sweets.
Her nose is a chocolate button
Her laugh, a gentle bleat.

Her eyes are two round caramels,
Her lips, a rosy smudge.
Her shoes are slippered liquorice,
Her mouth talks toffee fudge.

Ivan Jones

The Busy Head

There goes the head,
she's off like a rocket,
each eye like a Catherine wheel
revolving in its socket.

Superman can't touch her
as she whizzes round the school,
up and down the corridor
and in and out the hall,

all about the playground
and then upon the stage
with the vigour of a tiger
escaping from a cage.

She breaks the speed of sound
with a supersonic blast
and there's just a flash of light
to say the head's gone past.

She's the busiest person
in the school, it's true,
but there's one thing that I wonder –
what exactly does she do?

Charles Thomson

The Head's Hide-out

The head crouched in his hide-out
Beneath a dustbin lid.
"I want to see," he muttered,
"No teacher and no kid,

"No parent, no inspector,
Never a district nurse,
And, please, not one school dinner:
The things are getting worse!"

All morning, as the phone rang,
He hid away. Instead:
"The head is in the dustbin,"
The secretary said.

"The head is in the dustbin?"
"Yes, he'll be there all day.
He likes sometimes to manage
A little getaway.

"Last year he went to Holland.
Next year he's off to France.
Today he's in the dustbin.
You have to take your chance."

The head sprang from the garbage
As end-of-school came round.
He cried, "That's quite the nastiest
Hideaway I've found!

"I think I'll stick to teachers
And kids and parents too.
It's just sometimes I've had enough."
Don't blame him. Do you?

Kit Wright

Mr Body, the Head

Our Head, Mr Body, is six feet tall,
he's always on his toes and has a heart of gold.
He has a finger in every pie
and a chip on his shoulder.

He doesn't stand for any cheek
and so we don't give him any lip
– and we don't talk back.

Mr Body knows when we're pulling his leg
and he says, "Hold your tongue,
just you knuckle under and toe the line.
I want no underhand tricks here!"

He says our new school
cost an arm and a leg to build.
He had to fight for it tooth and nail.

Mr Body says he shoulders the burden of
   responsibility
and ends up doing the work of four people.
That must make him a forehead.

John Rice

How many parts of the body can you spot in this poem? If you
can spot 20 then give yourself a big hand!

School Calendar 6

We'll Never Live it Down!

Daffodil hats, bunny-eared bonnets,
Caps with beaks for peaks –
In Miss Meeny's art class
We've had two hilarious weeks.

We'd not have roared and giggled
If we'd guessed where it would lead
Or we'd have made them different –
Those hats – different indeed!

Now Miss insists we WEAR them...
She says we'll look *"So sweet!"*
What is more, OUTSIDE the school
Parading in the street!

Miss grinned that since we'd done so well
(Oh PLEASE don't come to gloat)
She got us *"luckily"* a place
Aboard an Easter float.

Philip Waddell

School Caretakers

The Lollipop Lady

When
we come to the
busy street we stand
beside the kerb and wait.
The lady with the lollipop
makes the teatime traffic stop.
When it's our turn to go across
even the hugest lorries pause.
Her lolly's like a magic wand —
cars bicycles and buses stand
and wait until we're over on
the other pavement. Once
we're gone the traffic
all begins to flow
but only
w
h
e
n
s
h
e
s
i
g
n
a
l
s
GO!

Pamela Gillilan

Nurse Greenaway
Understands

Wendy's wasp-sting,
Graeme's grazes,
Roisin's rash and
Sanjay's sneezes,

take them to Nurse Greenaway,
to soothe and smooth and clean away.

Bottles, ointments, sticky plasters,
ready for the worst disasters,
yet she rarely uses these,
on throbbing thumbs
or bloody knees.

Gentle words, with healing hands,
are Nurse G's kit. She understands.

Trisha's toothache,
Nichelle's nose,
Benjie's boil and
Tommy's toes,

take them to Nurse Greenaway,
to soothe and smooth.
She's seen a way,

but listens to each sobbing voice
and then explains her calming choice.
In Room A12 she's Queen, I'd say.
Yes, we all love
Nurse Greenaway.

Gentle words, with healing hands,
are Nurse G's kit. She understands.

Liz's split lip,
Tariq's thigh,
Eddie's ear and
Bab's black eye!

Take them to Nurse Greenaway,
to soothe and smooth and clean away.

Mike Johnson

First Taste of the School Dentist

I crossed the playground,
Past the conker championships
And people playing
Football on the drain.
I entered the school
And knew somehow
Something was different.
I walked up the corridor
Where the air smelled
Of washing-up liquid
And cough mixture.
I passed the playtime bell
And the coat-room.
Then there was a whisper:
"The dentist! The dentist is here."
I went to the classroom;
The whisper was there too:
"The dentist! The dentist is here."
The news hung in the room
Like a stencil drying
After printing.
Then the dentist called for me.
It looked at my teeth
With an eye on a stick.

Then it said, "You can go."
I never want to see
A dentist again;
Its eye tastes wrong!

Douglas Swinyard (12)

Old Boy

We had a visit the other day
from a world-famous footballer
who is a former pupil of our school.

The celebrity had agreed to open our new gym
and the head had said he was sure
such a distinguished visitor
would prove to be an inspiration to us.

This is how the great day went.

First our visitor,
especially known for his headers,
nodded off during the school assembly.

Later he visited each of our classrooms
giving us autographs with a borrowed pen,
actually my pen, which he failed to return.

Next he made an excuse
and disappeared to the toilets
where he was caught
(by Mr Blabbit)
having a forbidden smoke.

Finally, after he'd unveiled the plaque
inscribed with his name and the date,
he kicked a ball for the press photographers.
It was an impressive shot, really curved –
and straight through the glass of the staff-room
   window.

The next day in the paper
our head was quoted as saying,
"How refreshing to know that
some people can remain so unspoilt by fame.
In fact, our old boy hasn't changed a bit."

Philip Waddell

The Caretaker does his Job

Stop messing around.
Get out of the hall.
What are you doing
at this time in school?

No one should be in.
The head made it clear.
Stop dancing around
and come over here.

I saw you earlier
this afternoon.
You'll be in deep trouble
pretty soon.

Stop smirking like that
and give me your name.
I was young once –
I know your game.
You like to act bad,
then go off and boast.
Now where have you gone?
You're what?

...THE SCHOOL GHOST

Charles Thomson

School Calendar 7

All Fools' Day

First voice: Look you bicycle wheel
turning round!
When you look down
you feel like a clown.

Chorus: *Yay, Yay*
Today is All Fools' Day!

Second voice: Look you drop a penny
pon the ground!
When you think you lucky
and look down,
Not a thing like money
pon the ground.

Chorus: *Yay, Yay,*
Today is All Fools' Day!

Third voice: Look you shoelace loose out!
When you hear the shout
and look down at you shoe
It ain't true, it ain't true.

Chorus: *Yay, Yay,*
Today is All Fools' Day!

Fourth voice: Look you mother calling you!
Look you mother calling you!
Is true, is true, is true!

First voice: Well let she call till she blue
I ain't going nowhay.
You ain't ketching me this time
Today is All Fools' Day.

Mother's voice: Kenrick! Kenrick! Kenrrriicckk!
See how long I calling this boy
and he playing he ain't hear.
When he come I gon cut he tail!

John Agard

Everybody's Special Friend

Teacher's Rabbit

Whatever size
of hutch she's in,
whatever sort
or make or shape,
teacher's rabbit
has the habit
of trying to escape.

We all rush round
the playground in
a right old
hullabaloo –
look, there's the rabbit! –
quickly – grab it!
and in the end we do.

We put her back
inside the hutch,
nail wood, stretch wire
and wrap round tape,
but will her rabbit
stop her habit
of trying to escape?

Charles Thomson

The Class Guinea Pig

The earth does not shake
the stars do not make
a bow for the sake
of our guinea pig
who died today.
But still we cry,
as many tears as stars in the sky,
because everyone should know
how his little life was so
important to us.

Tim Pointon

Miss! Sue is Kissing

Miss! Sue is kissing
the tadpoles again.
She is, Miss. I did,
I asked her. She said
something about catching
him young. Getting one
her own age. I don't know,
Miss. She keeps whispering,
"Prince, Prince." Isn't that
a dog's name, Miss?

Michael Harrison

Rosie

Have you met our Rosie yet?
She's very, very sweet.
We love her from her round pink ears
Down to her tiny feet.
Be gentle, you can take her out –
She'll climb up on your shoulder.
And even Jake sits quiet when
He gets a turn to hold her.

Her whiskers are all twitchery
Around her pretty nose,
And it really, really tickles
When she crawls inside your clothes.
We like to share our snacks with her
(She's getting kind of fat).
She's everybody's special friend –
She's Rosie, our class rat.

Carol Diggory Shields

School Calendar 8

May Daze – or Henry, the Reluctant Maypole Dancer

My teacher told me yesterday
That Tracy Black would be away
(A skiddly-doo, a skiddly dee)
  On May Day.

We're one of those unbalanced classes
With sixteen lads and fourteen lasses
So who would partner Linda Grey
If Tracy Black was still away
(Dah-tiddly widdly doo)
  On May Day?

For every year upon the green
The girls would dance and choose a Queen
(Rumpty-tumpty tumty dum)
  On May Day.

When teacher asked the question who
Would fill the gap and see them through
There wasn't another lad in view
To join the dainty dancing crew
(Oh – leggit or bust, in a cloud of dust)
  On May Day.

I told her what me dad would say
But she took no notice anyway
She stood me next to Linda Grey
And told me I'd a part to play
  On May Day.

And diddly-diddly round we go
And what we're doing I'll never know
But we got our ribbons tangled so
And Linda Grey stood on me toe
(A-widdly doo, a widdly dee)
  On May Day.

The biggest crowd I'd ever seen
Assembled on that village green
You've never seen a crowd so keen
And who do you think they chose for Queen
(A skiddly diddly, oh! the pain)
  On May Day?

                                        Ian Whybrow

Our School Trip

Recipe for a Class Outing

Ingredients:
30 children, washed and scrubbed
29 packed lunches (no bottles)
3 teachers
an equal quantity of mums
1 nosebleed
2 fights
a hot day
3 lost purses
1 slightly torn dress
plenty of sweets
5 or 6 songs (optional)

Method:
Place children and adults in a bus and heat slowly.
Season well with sweets, reserving a few for later.
Heat to boiling point. Add fights and nosebleed.
Leave to simmer for 2 hours.

Remove children and packed lunches and leave to
   cool.
Stir in torn dress and lost purses.
Return to heat, add songs to taste.
Mix thoroughly. If the children go soggy and start
to stick together, remove from the bus and drain.
At the end of the cooking time divide into
   individual portions (makes about 36).
Serve with relief, garnished liberally with dirt.

Sue Cowling

School Visit to the Sculpture Park

"Don't touch! Don't touch!" the grown-ups glare.
"Don't tear the place apart.
Show some respect for the treasures here,
Don't you know it's ART?"

But
The children touch
And feel
And stroke
And probe
And explore it all.

The ballet-dancer's skirt of bronze
The baby's marble cheek
The sheep's rough woollen coat of stone
The boy's lean back of teak

The children touch
And feel
And stroke
And probe
And find it beautiful.

The teacher smiles, looks proudly round,
Explains it to the crowd.
"Permission to touch – that's what we've got,
For us, it *is* allowed!"

Jennifer Curry

Next!

Lining up in neat rows
standing two-by-two,
we all wait in silence
in that long and winding queue.

But it's not to see a statue
or get into a park,
it's not to see a museum
or a special work of art.

No, we're all lined up in rows
standing two-by-two,
waiting on our school trip
to use the one and only loo.

Andrew Collett

107

School Trip

I saw a man in a cardboard box
I saw a lady too,
Her head was wrapped in paper,
She only had one shoe.
We went and saw where Nelson is
We visited St Paul's,
We visited the Palace
and we climbed the city walls.

We saw the Tower Bridge open,
We went and saw Big Ben

... but I remember ladies
and boxes full of men.

Peter Dixon

School Calendar 9

Final Assembly

The long, last assembly of term:
hard floor, numb bums
and a one-man chat show
(that's the head!)

Miles of swimming certificates
to hand out, just for swimming
a tiddly few widths! Gee whiz!
Music awards, cycling awards,
(shuffles and yawns)
prizes for this, prizes for that –
it's a wonder there isn't
a prize for the caretaker's cat!

I'm usually brain-dead by now
but it's different today.
Our team's won the Cup.
It's there on the table,
gleaming and ribboned

and with it, somewhere,
(high up where I can't see)
is my medal
– first ever –
I can hardly wait for it to be me.

Patricia Leighton

It's Easy!

No Kidding?

"It's easy,"
said Mr Beasly
lean and
keen
hands
on hips
legs like
telegraph
poles   the high-jump rope
in his
black   "Right
Adidas   highered   next one,"
jogging   he said.
pants
then   he   "Do I have to, sir?"
with a glint in his eye   said titchy Ken.

Patricia Leighton

111

My Eyes are Watering

I've got a cold
And that is why
My eyes are watering.

It's nothing to do
With getting caught
When I had planned
To SMASH
The rounders ball
SO FAR
That it would go
Into PERMANENT ORBIT
Round the school.
It would've done, too –
If Lucy Smith
Hadn't RUSHED
To catch it.
"Look at Trevor –
He's having a cry!"
Not true.
I've got a cold
And THAT is why
My eyes are watering.

OK?

Trevor Harvey

Netball

When
trying
to score
at netball
it helps
if you're
more
than
usually
normally
excess-
ively
extra-
ordinar-
ily
tall.

Ann Bonner

Being Stuck in Goal

The goalie's ill,
Oh drat! I'm in goal.
Just my luck.
I've got the wind blowing in my face,
The ground's waterlogged
And it's near enough snowing.
All the play has been at the other end.
My hands are like ice-cubes.
I feel the bitter weather
Biting off one toe at a time.

Only a few minutes left,
And,
Suddenly,
They break,
Their best player is leading the attack,
He's shooting.
I summon up all my energy
And hurl myself across the goal
Landing with a thud.

It knocks me breathless
But I'm still clutching the ball.
Everybody is bundling me,
The team's hero.

Paul Oliffe (11)

Ms Jones, Football Teacher

Ms Jones,
  football teacher,
red shellsuit,
  flash boots.
She laughs
  as she centres,
shrieks "GOAL!"
  when she
    shoots!

Ms Jones,
  what a creature,
pink lipstick,
  shin-pads.
See there
  on the touchline
lots of
  bug-eyed
    lads.

Ms Jones'
  finest feature,
long blonde hair
  – it's neat.

She back heels
   and bend kicks;
she's fast
   on her
      feet.

Ms Jones,
   football teacher,
told us,
   "Don't give up!"
She made us
   train harder
and we
   won the
      Cup!

Wes Magee

Beware!

The crocodile is coming!
It's heading for the pool,
It's swaying down the road
From the local Primary School.
Better keep your distance,
Better close your doors –
Beware the fearful clamour
From its ever-open jaws!
Be careful not to stumble
As you hurry from the street:
Remember that the crocodile
Has sixty trampling feet!
Through the city jungle
The creature marches on.
Wisely, shoppers stand aside
And wait until it's gone.
It's going to cross the busy street –
It starts to leave the path –

Attacked by snarling traffic
It's completely cut in half –
The head continues on its way,
The tail, delayed, just laughs
And runs to catch it up
At the Municipal Baths.
The crocodile is swimming
In the Public Swimming Pool,
But soon it will be heading
For the local Primary School.
So, better keep your distance,
Better if you try
To find a place to hide
While the crocodile goes by!

June Crebbin

Sports Day

Oh no! My race next.
We're all in a line.
I'm about to be sick.
Now the countdown,
O-o-o-n-n your marks,
G-e-e-t-t set,
Go!
And we're off.

First of all my friend is in the lead,
Then I'm catching up on her,
We're getting equal,
Now I've got the edge,
I'm away on my own,
Down on the finish,
Two more steps to go,
I look around,
I'm way ahead,
The last step.

A-a-n-d-d I've finished.

Phew! What a race, what a lead.
It must have been a record.
Wow! It IS a record!
All I can hear in the background
Is the loudspeaker
Shouting the news. What a win!

Grace Mason (14)

School Calendar 10

First Day of the Holidays

It's early

My body is heavy and relaxed.
My tousled head, warm in the hollow of the
pillow.
My eyes feel delightfully fresh and cool.

It's excitement.

A bubbling underground spring,
longing to burst free,
to express effervescently the undiscovered.

It's ecstasy.

Like the birth of a sneeze.
The sparkling crest of a yawn.
The calm after spasms of perpetual hiccups.

I stretch.
And throw wide my sunfilled curtains of happiness.

Nikki Field (13)

Acknowledgements

The compiler and publishers would like to thank the
following for permission to use copyright material in
this collection. The publishers have made every effort
to contact the copyright holders but there are a few
cases where it has not been possible to do so. We
would be grateful to hear from anyone who can enable
us to contact them so that the omission can be cor-
rected at the first opportunity.

John Agard for "All Fools' Day" from *I Din Do Nuttin*, pub.
The Bodley Head, by kind permission of Caroline Sheldon
Literary Agency ~ Daniel Bishop for "Giggles" from
Wondercrump Poetry, pub. Random House Children's Books
~ Sue Cowling for "Recipe for a Class Outing" from *What
is a Kumquat*, pub. Faber & Faber ~ June Crebbin for
"Beware!" from *The Jungle Sale*, pub. Viking Kestrel, 1988 ~
Jennifer Curry for "Infant Art" and "School Visit to the
Sculpture Park", and for "Ten Cornflowers" by Jenny Craig
~ Kalli Dakos for "A Teacher's Lament" from *If You're Not
Here, Please Raise Your Hand*, reprinted with the permission
of Simon & Schuster Books for Young Readers, an imprint
of Simon & Schuster Children's Publishing Division ~ Peter
Dixon for "Colour of my Dreams", "Nativity Play" and
"School Trip" from *Lost Property Box (Sandwich Poets)*, pub.
Macmillan ~ Mick Gowar for "Fruit" and "New Leaf" from
Third Time Lucky, pub. Viking Kestrel, 1988 ~ Michael

Harrison for "Miss! Sue is Kissing" from *Junk Mail*, pub. OUP, 1993 ~ Mike Johnson for "Nurse Greenaway Understands" from *Who Rules the School*, ed. Paul Cookson, pub. Macmillan, 1988 ~ Ivan Jones for "Miss Sweet and Sour" ~ Grace Mason and James Allen's Girls' School for "Sports Day" ~ Judith Nicholls for "Storytime" from *Midnight Forest*, and for "Late" from *Mirror Mirror*, both pub. Faber & Faber ~ Gareth Owen for "Conversation Piece" reproduced by permission of Rogers, Coleridge & White Ltd ~ Brian Patten for "Schoolitis" and "How the New Teacher got her Nickname" from *Thawing Frozen Frogs*, Viking, 1990 ~ Turning Heads Poetry & Theatre Co for "The Truant"; "There's Someone in our Class" by Marcus Throup; "Photographs" by Nicholas Grant; "Emma and Rebbecca" by Kelly Bambrick; "Quarrel" by Jeremy Consitt; "Being Stuck in Goal" by Paul Oliffe and "First Day of the Holidays" by Nikki Field ~ To PJ Walsh for "Paul's Flowers" by John Walsh from *Poets in Hand*, pub. Puffin Books ~ Dave Ward for "Jazzz Watches Candy do her Homework" from *Candy and Jazzz*, pub. OUP ~ Kit Wright for "The Head's Hide-out" from *Cat Among the Pigeons*, pub. Viking Kestrel, 1987 Benjamin Zephaniah for "Serious Luv" from *Funky Chickens*, pub. Viking, 1996